Edge of Feedback

A semi-autobiographical short story

by

Steve Jones

Published by New Generation Publishing in 2020

First Edition

ISBN 978-1-80031-718-5

www.newgeneration-publishing.com

The Edge of Feedback

Part 1

There is some dark treacle. From nowhere in particular it runs slowly covering the head, slug slow, snide and sly, it runs like no other depression, this is new; every black dog visit is a breed apart from the last one.

I slip on a CD to fight back, swig deep at the blue bottled neck of 7.5% apples. The dight is nark, and the guitar solo voice of Dawn Upshaw and the Sorrowful Songs wretches the whole shed, grinds me through the coffee, wakens me once again to the suffering of man. It's not necessarily a black thing, an African American thing, this blues; this wringing out of the soul is a curse, blessed upon those whose cup runneth over with sensitivity. An inner urge to scream at the moon and shout, "*here I am, I feel, I AM HURTING!*"

Forty seven years have slithered past, back in the seventies I was bursting with envy.

The common room in our Secondary School reeked of aching sex. We lads thought that blues rock LP albums tucked under our arms were a sure way to get the girls roadying behind us like some gormless models in a cigar advert. So the thing was to keep either a Led Zeppelin album or Cream's Disraeli Gears LP somewhere inside the anorak, parka, or worn leather satchel and sandwich box heap of the neo hippy self.

I begged and sulked and repeated the servility and mood until an Aunt gifted to me an electric guitar and amp. It was at this time of life-seventeen-going on twenty six that I took an interest in philosophy. I put some stuff into practice. Most problems in life can be solved once a pattern has been established. So I studied my parents and neighbours patterns of lifestyle. There was a definite absence of these people on a Tuesday afternoon between

3.45pm after school, until 5.52. I played the guitar loud and on the edge of feedback.

The late sixties proved to be sexual awakeness time. On the cusp of having to leave school I was sort of panicing. I had a crush on a few girls and the ones I crushed on were as my Dad said "the tart type" I couldn't abide the straight laced Janets and Gillians of the world, but fancied Jennifer the venial and Mary Anne Bikesheds- the smoker sensual. Wisps of tobacco smoke drifted from between her ruby red pursed lips and drove me sad. So the longing for a first sexual encounter and the temptation of heavy rock with its string bending and impending inevitably the sound filled my stomach where until this day it remains pushed down.

The blues ferments forever; never brews out, one stirs out of bed with the song in the head and rests in bed at night exhausted and in sleep we wrestle with microphones and Wah! Wah! pedals and screw hard the girl who never materialises. The very act of retiring, the ripping off of a tee shirt and thumbs pressing down onto belted Levi's stirred the young inexperienced pink trombone to attention.

As I self-exiled in my parents box room, second hand record player, turntable spinning, arm and needle surfing the sound waves I thought of Girls. One cannot *save* up for a girlfriend, even so, at one shilling a week, "ho hum!"

My friend James, he was tall and all legs and a cheeky bastard had a girl for every foyer.

Flavoured crisps had just come on the scene, salt and vinegar. James seduced girls with crisps, chewing gum and his football shorts. In turn I offered nothing but shyness, shyness my first taste of the blues, manifesting itself in the tracks of Sunshine of your Love, and One Inch Rock by Tyranosaurus REX.

At discos and common room functions I would press myself to walls, or sit in corner thinking only of chat up lines. From previous experience I knew that my advance would be drowned out by a lead break or disc jockey outburst, leaving me so upstaged and laughable, - sulking into the shadows.

But there was one girl who had captured me throughout fourth year. Classes had amalgamated to form common subjects. CC sat at the back of every classroom on our semi chore daily reluctance - prancing from one lesson to the next. She was long black haired with curls and high cheekbones gypsy eyed and sultry. It was this girl above all that I've previously mentioned I loved. I thought of her as being miles above my station, I followed her home, we spoke, became friends.

Within days I had abandoned the Blues, listened to the Beatles and the Beachboys...good vibrations.

It was with James at the back of the bike sheds that I tried my first cigarette. I pulled a fag from a pack he said his mother wouldn't miss. The conversation went like this.

"Hey Steve!"

"Yeah!"

"See that girl over there?"

He pointed to my new friend CC

"what about her?"

"Fucked her last night, never again she's weird"

A lump came in my throat, I loved James, he shot from the hip, and if he bragged about anything, it was true; he was not a bull-shitter…so I was lost for tears.

"Why wouldn't you go out with her again?" I whimpered

James drew deeply on his fag and poured verbal bleach over my feelings for the girl.

"She wouldn't let me put it all in, only the end, only the end …..like my brother does she said!"

CC had an older brother; he was handsome and left the school a year ago.

The realisation of ones naivety, that my perception of the way the world worked, the way humans integrated, and my ignorance of financial attraction and craving flared up in my brain like some threatening disease.

I crawled back into the box room, out came Led Zeppelin and Lady Chatterley. D H Lawrence was my first rude book, and I quickly soaked up his mind set. Lawrence was an angry man, he was not afraid to scald the Christian, pour verbal subterfuge over common values. If I was ever to stroke a girl on each hip, I needed to know what a girl was, how they viewed us boys, and what they wanted, so I could give the right stuff. Jimi Hendrix helped in many ways. His guitar playing and the cover of his album "Electric Ladyland" drew me into the lyrics, lyrics so poetic and sensual I was hooked at first listen. I needed to know what made this musician great so I could cream off a bit and use it on girls.

My aunt booked and paid for three guitar lessons for me. I attended *one* lesson.

"Steven is tone deaf, has no idea of the concept of musical language, I have to be brutally honest"

I picked up my second hand guitar, cream valve baked amp and sulked back to my aunts car, was dropped off at home, hardly a word spoken. I was a waste of time, a waste of money, and tone fucking deaf in the space of two hours.

I was aiming to help my opposite sex attractiveness by swinging a guitar from my shoulder, now my parents put an advert in the shop for the gear.

The lesson, never speculate about ones potential until you have proven to yourself that there's a slim chance you may possess it.

I sulked in the tiny box room cell, and thought of death.

Another lesson, "never do things for the wrong reasons" at 17 years, I began to realise that life was a minefield. I was a slow person. James my mentor seemed to have all the knowledge of how to get by, built in. I was paddling frantically, needed a girl; that much I knew, but above all, School was coming to an end. I was at a loss to choose a career.

I thought I was a reasonable artist, a fair painter, but with the recent failures with girls and music, my confidence began to syphon off. I started to drink and think of CC. Why had she favoured James, and what was that thing with her brother. My mother slapped me hard in that box room, "stop dwelling!" and the door slammed and I knew this was a warning. I had to grip the real world… feed myself; it was holding me back this damn immaturity!

***

Now I sit as often as not in a shed. My work life all but ended. I sit dry and bleached like an old snail shell. There's no moisture left inside. No hopes, no fears. I have had a reasonable innings. The blues remain however; they have been faithful all these years, fiftyish in all. My long suffering wife deserves some kind of an award for bravery; our three married children, an award for endurance. 2016, and write this listening to Hawkwind, Silver Machine 1972. Forty four years since intense "Dirty Ducking." I have recently become aware that I am no longer thinking of sartorial presentation. I have given up using masculine anti- aging creams and tooth whitener. My attention at the Barbers now focused purely on price and the hairdresser's breasts. It doesn't matter about the cranium presentation. From a respectable round face that lasted quite a few years jowls hang in the sink whilst shaving. A beer belly competes. I look ridiculous in jeans and trainers, look too retired working class in a suit, too pretentious when I wear my Fedora and national socialist when I don my national health tortoise shell round spectacles. I made a special journey to London many years ago to purchase the glasses from a specialist shop in Covent Garden….I have only wore them a few times, the lens prescription having expired.

My blues now has a competitor-depression.

I have always harboured a will to be different. I tried the Scouts and Air Cadets but uniforms I could not stomach. Two of our three children joined the forces, the third is a Chef. They went through all the emotions I felt during childhood and puberty and thankfully none of them exhibited a rebellious streak. Our family survival philosophy is so easy going; there was nothing to rebel against. I often wonder if the two offspring who joined the forces really needed to experience the sensations of discipline. My wife and I being laid back and accommodating encouraged the kids in whatever, whenever.

As open minded as I was I admit that it never occurred to me to ask the children at *their* vulnerable time - the transition from schooling to work - about their anxieties. My wife and I never took them to one side and gave sex and financial advice. We let them stagger as bewildered as we did into the mayhem of reality. I regret this deeply. There is so much we didn't help them with just because we had stumbled too. Suddenly it's too late.

***

I left school after the fourth year. My results were so poor that I never picked up the CSE certs. There were only two half decent ones only, Technical drawing and Art. My excuse was due to illness and a mind that wondered my heart was dedicated to sensual experience rather than study. My father wanted me to work at his foundry; my grandfather had worked there too. Mother knew I had an interest in books and arty farty stuff. She brushed me down and took me to the employment office in Walsall. Two jobs were up for interview. A Dental Technician and a trainee draughtsman, within a few weeks I secured the trainee draughtsman job.

Just across the road and in view of my drawing board was a boozer-The Falcon. Only ten minutes' walk down into Walsall there was another pub called the Dirty Duck. These two places being opposite ends of the drinking market-old and young played a devastating part in my life.

I have lost quite a lot of my writing from the seventies. I recently found a biro defiled copy of March Battalion by

Sven Hassel, my habit then and still, no matter how virginal the book I always used any blank spaces to catch my mental semen.

This is one such spurt;-

Her little fickle fingers,
Flirted with her hair,
While from her all-consuming eyes,
Blasted urgent, a flaming stare.

It was aimed at a chip shop girl Lidia. I chose her as my imaginary girlfriend. The chip shop was Siamese to The Falcon pub and just a blink from my drawing board; I had sight and sighs of her helping to set up the chippy an hour before it was due to open. I watched with sullen heart her hard working arms and pretentious customer smile. Lidia was blonde, had green eyes, baby like yours, baby like yours, a Woodstock doll. My pencil pressed hard in urgency onto parchment held by pins and masking tape. My mind raced and traced in haste to rush over to her and…

"Small chips please Lidia!"

And the sickly grins of our mutual acknowledgement… that I was too timid to ask her out, signed the chip paper that started a war. A war of blubbered words, never fired, fell like vinegar into my pithy bag of chips; for many months my heart ached until she was pulled by a plumber friend who asked and got what he wanted.

Henceforth I viewed and pressed my dismay into a few words which I'd recently found….a bank for emotions; The *Stoical* Bank of Steve the suppressed.

***

It is my 64th year to heaven and apologies Dylan Thomas but you wished your words to be remembered, and I am bastardizing them, singing your song, playing with your words, trashing your excellent syntax. I am experiencing difficulty coming out of the molasses of this depression. A sharp hail shower shatters the silent shed and I look out of the window. I see millions of doomed diamonds and realise my own mortality and the dog pulls and I heave back, my arms struggle to orchestrate the shed. Pour a drink, choose a track, adjust the volume, take a swig, sit down, stand up, run fingers through a despair of my hair, tidy cassettes, deal with CD's feel through my trousers my thinning knees and nothing…absolutely nothing is helping me to dodge dark thoughts, nothing, nothing, I am helpless, a mind full of memories, a mind full of regret and I'm stuck with the fucking thing…its tinnitus plus never ending questioning and self-criticism is driving me sad. Driving me sad… and I'm black and blue, black and blue, all is damn black and blue!

I pull hard on the glass of recollections the same old 7.5% apples, and expect stupidly, a different outcome from all the other lost nights of drinking and brain shrinking all the time knowing it, but never mention all stinks with dementia.

I wish I were as quick as a Blue Tit, as easy as a snake, determined as a spider. I wish too much, hope too often, but my life! a bloody good book is hard to put down. I go over it like a BBC Editor, but one cannot edit a POLLOCK. Whether or not you're from Jackson or Walsall, there's no undoing, no matter how I try I cannot placate ghosts of the past. When I use "fuck" uncharacteristically (I find I am doing this with ever increasing regularity) I know I am ill.

I am among absent friends when I play a CD of blues. I sit in a scene ripped right from Les Miserables where damp empty chairs and empty tables where my thoughts will sit no more, mock knowing that they will fucking outlast me… ya bastards.

Modern day blues I think is less severe. Every local blues concert I attend, the age group appears to be the same.. 50s to 70 years of age. So the 60s kids lament has a pattern. We crave for mortal coil renewal.

Young folk, (unless it's me) – are now wrapped up in technology, there's a lot more stuff to look forward to after work, the ether of life is heavy with the distracted souls of individualism, and I think this is a shame.

A recent soul on the scene is Sea Sick Steve, an ex-hobo. Since being talent spotted by an eminent musician, Sea Sick Steve has shot to fame. He brings his street raw blues to the young at open and closed air concerts. Steve is an old bloke, a Kerouac character, his life, like the unorthodox string instruments he plays has been contrived. Edith Piaf and SSS will shake hands and embrace on the other side of life. Sorry Steve, but your music brings no ghosts back, but it sooths my black and blue skin.

Oh! Fela Kuti, you've just fell as a result of music vibrations, from the shed apex shelf, hit my head and landed on my balls, lap licking and political, I will play you… now you've asked, Shuffering and Shmiling for 12:20secs. Sorry about your Mother.

I have been long jealous of this long dead African musician/revolutionary.

Another half-litre of apples. My body begins to loosen up, mind too. Now a long way from my dwelling lachrymose real self, I can now let in the history again, and in it comes, love, hatred, lust, politics, competition, and a yearning to say sorry to those who I offended, ignored and gave immature advice to….and it remains as was, is now, and will be for evermore. Hang on some sane self, hang on to the Summer Breeze - it will make me feel fine, blowing in the Jasmine of my mind, thanks to The Islay Brothers.

In the early seventies I was not cognisant of the impact ones social and IQ standing had on future prosperity. I had a rival. A well-educated lad Murphy started the same day as me… we sat swivelling on our drawing board high chairs taking in the rules of design for our chosen industry. Murphy was extremely bright and remains so until this day. We both came from a working background. I quickly fell victim to his superior intellect. I envied him his quick uptake regarding engineering. It soon transpired that we had only one thing in common….drinking. I drank heavily to suppress my fear of entering into a world where I felt intellectually challenged. My naivety knew no bounds. In the Falcon at lunchtime Murphy and I were buddies, equally skilled at piss taking, dominoes, darts and downing pints. At work, Murphy excelled at mathematics quickly solving the most complex of hydraulic calculations. I however had the edge on design and overall drawing presentation. Murphy was a soul music fan, and I must admit that I liked very much his taste in music especially Motown. His choice of music soul and Status Quo was very popular. Murphy was tall, sporty and smart. It was a tough few years. I struggled to keep up intellectually. He read Homer and Agatha Christie. Murphy helped me with the Daily Mirror crossword, showed me how to look deep into the cryptic clues. I was in awe of the guy. We had fundamental differences though. I was champing at the bit for a girl; Murphy was a realist, a fatalist. So I deserted him, began to let him down at the Falcon working class blokes pub, I struck out for The Dirty Duck. I begged Murphy to come along. He was obviously more mature than I. I started to drink Barley Wines in the Dirty Duck, fell into the arms of a Gypsy eyed girl, we rocked to Lenard Skinnard, Pink Fairies, Pink Floyd, Uriah Heap, Hendrix and Derek and the Dominoes. The Gypsy and I fucked, ate hot dogs, chips and stroked each other on each hip until our brains went soft.

Ted Heath declared a three day week and there was a fuel shortage; Middle East crisis, ration books for fuel. The Gypsy and I used our days off work to bath fuck ourselves silly until all fingers and toes were lined with the soak syndrome.

On one occasion, her pregnant next door neighbour, Murphy played darts, got himself a part time job in the chip shop, and steamed ahead of me financially and maturely. I had a girl, I had a girl, I was having sex, Murphy was watching ‘x’ rated films. I did everything he passed on from this. On one occasion, our noisy bath time marathons prompted a neighbour to knock on the door and express envy and to keep the verbal's down.

***

I pull hard using all my tenuous will power. I struggle to regain my robbed sanity. I look up from my computer screen and see my dusk self-reflected in the shed window. I hate the self I see. It looks face filled and double chinned, so stoical, so unfeeling the realisation of this is terrifying, I don't really like the person in the reflection, and I am appalled at what it has become. I am a poor excuse for the efforts of regeneration, a disappointment for ancestors.

I have faults. One has been poisoning me for many years. I could stop the gulps at the drop of a pin. I prefer however to run with this one as my poison awakens the real guy within.

The shed grows dim, wooden sharp edges glow gilt and palatial. My reflection stubbornly hangs there framed by a dusty dusk window-all is la Bette noir.

I need closure on some acts and scenes of my… and instantly it comes…

Man born of woman has but a short time to live….

When we are children the life length appears eternal and then dulled by responsibility of feeding oneself, and the detritus of world affairs…the span has gone…and no one has ever said that a mistake is for ever…for ever…for ever. Naivety is a curse.

CC, my first love was innocent. She was coy. When she cried as we sat on the park bench talking about the James incident, her tears produced the sound of rain on rose petals.

And now she undoubtedly has forgotten. James and I met by coincidence at the Dirty Duck in Walsall. We exchanged pleasantries; he was a Building Clerk, still single. I tackled him regarding his confession-his boast of having made love to CC with the "just in" reference to CC's preference of intercourse.

“What was CC’s Brothers name Jonesy?”

“Errr…Justin…

“You’re slow!”

“Think about it!”

I was both gutted and ashamed when I worked it out. I had dumped my goddess…dumped her because of a damn joke which I was apparently too thick to pick up on. How fucking funny is that? The whole chemistry of attraction destroyed by a few words meant to trick, intellectually engineered to make fun of. Fuck, Fuck, Fuck!

The Beatles; I thought too pop. I began to listen to tracks from the White Album, Let It Be and other recordings.

While my guitar gently Weeps.

The Long and winding Road.

I Will.

Julia.

My parents were really pissed off overhearing night after night minor chords but I played and sulked on. I was having regular sex, the Gypsy was all powerful….but…and I couldn’t figure it out...but I knew.

Gypsy and I often gate crashed a darts match where Murphy was present. He seemed to warm to her and I tried to imagine what my life would be like if I split with her and Murphy picked up where I left off.

Murphy had intuition as well…I began to hate clever fuckers!

I began to loathe my dimness. I had proved myself capable of securing a future in design. I dressed smart, kept good time and was genuinely interested in engineering systems I designed. Self-doubt should have diminished here. But here I am forty 47 years on continuing to question my self-worth. I love winter months. Time in the shed brings another dimension, daytime is the agony of responsibility and creeping reflection. There are three deaths; the physical, the burial, and the last time anyone speaks your name. This I heard on a dream disturbed night while the World Radio filled my mind with a multitude of worries. The Gypsy was hot. I felt deep down that I couldn't keep up with her. My parents hated the whole infusion. The demand for sex and drink was distorting my limited vision for securing my future. But the times we were living in had some responsibility for this. Early seventies, ever closer to Nuclear conflict, Vietnam and the College film, "Survive and Protect", and the TV film, "When the Wind Blows" increased my mental sadness. Hedonism to me- "Mr Thicko" was the option.

The Doors.

"The End"

The general theme to "Apocalypse Now" was a tune ever revolving in my head. It had an effect on everyone in our office but was mostly unspoken. We plodded on from one crisis to another but most of all sex hang ups where questioned; girls and boys with the pill liberating both, began to ease up and talk freely about what was important and what was out of bounds in a sexual relationship. The Gypsy and I had no hang ups. We watched films Murphy invited us to view via spooling…in a room over a pub. The Gypsy and I were open minded, we both were as mad as a box of frogs. There was this nagging thought. I couldn't keep up, and I began to listen to friends and family, taking in their criticisms.

Murphy was directing me toward books he had read and studied in high school. I found that I had missed something massive having a secondary school education. I enjoyed the work of every author he had enthused about. I even reciprocated. I suggested stuff that I had discovered as offshoots to his favourite genre. We steamed together designing fire systems and discussing literature. But I felt a tug of loyalty. I had to make some decisions. As the boss said, I wasn't taking my future seriously. This assessment coupled with my friends and family comments turned up my mental wattage.

I chose hedonism over respectable responsibility.

I assumed that I may be bought back into the shared lime light if I passed my driving test (It was essential to further progression in our trade). Murphy as far as I was aware had not considered this. I was learning fast and decided albeit Murphy and I shared our personal thoughts and anxieties I would pursue this goal without comment. Every weekend my father and uncle put me through hell with slaps thumps and questions and I failed my first test. I immediately re applied, and within a few weeks, re took the test and passed. My mind was forever focused on sex and drink. Work being a means to an end so to speak.

Murphy had left his wage slip uncovered on his desk whilst he was out the back of the office smoking.

I did not touch it but looked and as I suspected, there was a considerable difference between or wages. So I counted my blessings, I had other assets, a girl who was popular tremendously, a driving license an old car which I was allowed to claim expenses for on trips for the company. The powers that be trusted me to work self-motivated. I saw less of Murphy.

Murphy was still to be envied though. He was fit, loved sport, tall thin and well dressed. In conversation with our clients he used words that I had to look up, like erudite, or cognisant. He also sported a full head of hair, beard and moustache and resembled a Musketeer. I knew he was quietly competitive and long awaited his presentation of a driving licence but this I learned he had put on a back burner. I thought this was a big mistake on his part and I felt satisfied.

Not for long though. Murphy's designs were based upon architectural drawings sent in by post…no surveys required. I was saddled with most of the trip out surveys that took time; cotton mills, tanneries, shoemakers etc. Every building being historical had to be measured accurately on site, sketched and then transposed onto large parchment drawing sheets. Murphy's output far exceeded mine as he was office based. His salary increased to the point where he never questioned the price of beer and sandwiches or the cost of a suit. He strolled into success and he deserved it. My naivety knew no bounds. I was on a constant treadmill trying to keep up and much more.

Trying too hard has always been my downfall. But trying too hard paddling in a different direction to other folk was never hinted at by others. I was Steve, and Steve does it his way and won't stop until he comes up for air and discovers he's on the bottom of the lake and not the surface.

Again I bumped into James. He had put on weight. We talked at length. He had studied and consequently been upgraded to a QS, put down a deposit on a house, his girlfriend was expecting and they had a marriage booked a couple of Months hence. We walked from the Dirty Duck laughing and joking, I thanked him for his verbal Wedding invitation and after we shook hands, he pulled keys from his pocket and unlocked a parked car, an MG - in British Racing Green. My Heart sank, I never did go to his wedding, firstly, I had had a crush on the girl he was marrying, second-my MG jealousy, and third, he had entered a most respected career in the building trade-a QUANTITY SURVEYOR.

Fair play James…that's what being mature is all about. I sank into a morbid depression.

"Murphy?"

"Steve?"

"What does rhetoric mean?"

"Flamboyant bullshit!" said Murphy.

The answer suggested that I needed to look it up for myself. I needed to grow up and work hard, study, calm down. But at the end of the day I was forever wrestling with reality and responsibility *and* what I thought was a secret pact between intellectuals-that of ridiculing secondary intelligent folk, people like me who didn't know shit.

So I listened to Fleetwood Mac, relaxed to their superb composition - Albatross, I sank into a Belly Dancers stomach undulations as she twisted slowly to the music of Santana, Samba Patti.

If I were to pull myself together, save money, ask the Gypsy for her hand in marriage, secure a mortgage and try for a family at least I would be keeping up somewhat in the mature sensible stakes. But there was a big problem. First I wasn't ready for the long haul. Second I was way behind in the savings stakes and third, the Gypsy who was younger than me had mega hedonistic tendencies. I was at a loss as to how to break these problems down into their component parts. There was a pattern here. I knew something had to drastically change. I grew desperately morose. I was cognisant that I had the strength to steer the ship of doom from the rocks but morbidly I wanted the experience of letting things deteriorate for the sheer hell of it. At the worst I was at risk of losing everything. As a result of this self-examination my first symptom of depression showed its teeth. I became withdrawn. Her gypsy eyes began to wonder. My boss and parents passed comment on my sartorial decline. I drank like a fish and my bank often bounced cheques. I was in love with life, but as it *could* be not as it was. I lacked the *Character* with which my friends and work colleagues had so easily portrayed. One by one they secured themselves a place in respectable society.

I was as this stage really fucking lost and too proud to ask for help.

I lay on her belly, she lay on mine. She was young and extremely vulnerable. We shared the fire and passion of the times. We didn't have a bean between us; lived from one pay day to the next. I suspect that sharing circumstances like this was similar to a botanist placing seeds in a warm hot environment. There was an inevitability that our passion in poverty would grow into love and maturity.

I listened avidly to a group called Judas Priest. The few lyrics I remember…Run of the Mill.

What have you achieved now that you're old?
Did you fulfil ambition, do as you were told
Or are you doing the same this year,
Should I give sorrow, or turn round and sneer.

This was at the age of twenty two. Not old, but an old head, cognisant of a lack of life understanding and too possessed of an incendiary passion to see clearly.

I pull away from this page. I pull my mind and body back into the shed. I can re live the senses of some forty plus years ago, hear the heavy rock and blues as it crawls from the Dirty Duck. I see dim sensuous bars, smell beer and grass, taste Barley Wine, and touch the pale skin which was hers, the gypsy.

***

I self-criticise. In this 64th year to oblivion I am a husk of a man. Eaten away by self-doubt and tired of cross examination. But it has had its rewards. Angry at the jovial and very loud noise from neighbours children whilst I write. I was on the verge of complaining. Now following a quick pause I am content with the distraction. My anger is caused by a gap in my life; our three children have grown up and gone away. We tend to keep in touch via technology. I have grown old and yearn for how things *where* and at loss to appreciate how things *are;* not to mention worried and pensive seeing the tunnel of darkness approaching; this vision coming up through train window eyes.

So I rest my guitar on my knee. Thanks to the same technology which I despise, I can blag the tuning via an inbuilt device. I can hear the resonance and sustained ping of strings being stretched into harmony. Tone deaf or not I can walk the frets with ease and hold down a dozen chords or so. Age finds me struggling with memory, I grow angry with myself, and at the back of my mind I worry about dementia having witnessed the same symptoms my mother did before she was diagnosed with Alzheimer's disease.

I strum a bluesy E, followed by A, an optimistic G and D, pauses briefly for an Am, and back again. The blues is mastered (like riveting writing) in my head on what is not said. Better to pull and push the strings to accentuate the cry into a wail.

Please Lord; desist from taking me whilst I burn with energy and passion. Take me when I have played a few songs, have some compassion for a man who has looked up in admiration at a real artist on a stage.

Take me when all the rage has gone and only melancholy lingers on.

And down again my head goes into the great screen of technology and my past.

Back then in my tumultuous hedonism I cried out for stability, I knew what was required of me.

A steady job

A female

A Mortgage…death debt

A Home

A will to strive for promotion and more money

With exception of the *female* part of the list anything else was not part of the agenda. I knew it had to be and desperately needed a hint of that illusive self-discipline, a will to take on responsibility. No matter how I tried I could not find this. It required a personality in total contrast to mine. I could not be ruthless. I *needed* to be ruthless. Being a gentle naïve guy I wasn't cut out for coping with brutal reality.

The Gypsy was causing a lot of problems for me. We were addicted to each other. She was hell fire and brimstone; I was lustful and lived for the day.

How the hell could I break away? We both tried dumping each other but parting lasted for a few hours only and we ran back crying and promising, crying and promising. The situation was exhausting. The gypsy had no idea of how I felt. I wanted her but she was out of control. If there were to be a future together I would have to brook the entire responsible bit myself. As it was I found myself exhausted, unable to break away, no courage to say enough is enough. So we carried on together drinking, dining and fucking, drinking dining and fucking. Something had to happen to break the cycle.

She had *let me touch her perfect body with my mind*. And so to close this chapter of my life, there is only one song, Suzanne, Leonard Cohen.

The overall power of ones parents over their mature children when it comes to the possibility of choosing a mate is quite devastating.

My relationship with the Gypsy came to an end when it became a choice, an abrupt ultimatum; a roof over my head or homelessness; it was as simple as that. That was the harsh reality.

Honour thy Father and thy Mother; that thy days may be long in the land which the Lord thy God giveth thee.

***

There is a group. They go by the name of Mostly Autumn. They are very beautiful people being talented songwriters and instrumentalists. Mostly Autumn are likened to Pink Floyd, but they stand out on their own using sentimental soul searching lyrics. I am listing to some tracks of theirs as I write this. The shed window reflects what I can only describe with my first mind- a dusk of urine yellow. The garden vista for late April 16 is very disappointing. It bounces back into my eyes like this song, "Questioning Eyes", deep, yearning, reaching out for that ultimate orgasm; a pushing to blossom.

I see the garden with all its potential to flourish, being capped with the circumstances of weather. I can empathise with the sensation. I write to dispel my fear of nothingness. I write to mark the earth with my presence in time. I write to share, but there's nobody there, nobody…not a fucking soul.

I am dismayed by the prospect of finding myself doomed to the three deaths, three stages of goodbye and oblivion. Creativity escapes me. A creation is only recognised and made eternal depending upon its value to future generations. My GP of 28 years recently retired. No official announcement. He just vanished from the face of my life. He was *something* to me, obviously this was not picked up by him, a little note at the surgery would have been good. Nothing…..all the help he gave folk.

"From today Mr Jones you will be under Doctor"…ok we jump off one bus and bounce upon another-better that way.

I had no courage to kiss goodbye to the Gypsy. I did the cowardly thing to save myself. I hid until she hated me. The best thing I thought to cauterize the emptying feeling - love bleeding to death.

It is extremely difficult to pull oneself from the quicksand of nostalgia.

I spent months after the split in solitary dark self-indulgence.

My boss asked me into his office. He didn't beat around the bush. I had to pull my socks up, get over it and start to think of my future with the company

"As it stands Steve, you're not making any headway; the next warning will be a written one!"

Of course Murphy may have been privy to the warning. I had for a long time shown the office nothing but my weakness for hedonism. I disciplined myself and was committed to a long haul to gain back respect for my designs. I sulked in secret; my heart broken.

Forty odd years later I am sitting in a shed. My wife is at work. It is late, she works shifts. I am presently winding down for retirement. I'm going through a bad stage. I am cognisant that as far as work is concerned that once again I'm treating it with contempt. The very craft that I have used to help raise family, pay for a house, finance holidays and hobbies has become a chore. I can no longer bear it. I am worn and utterly defeated. We are crumbling. The slightest wind will reduce us to sand. I sought out my ex school mate James. He, his wife, his children and life style are very polished accomplished. I envy James. He and his wife CC have not been distracted by the pull; the pull of romanticism.

Following long sessions of blues LP playing in particular John Mayall, Rolling Stones, I began to go out a bit and read books on philosophy and classic writers. These lonely reading sessions were taken after dinner, following a wash and change, in a Pub called the Elms in Aldridge.

It was during one of these sessions that a girl turned up and introduced herself to me. She had responded to a lonely hearts advertisement I had placed in a local newspaper.

She was shy. She was tiny, she had a wonderful smile and was henceforth destined to date a mad bloke and give birth to three great children.

My train journey now reaching its termination is giving me but a short time to repent. The slowing down, the clackety clack, clackety clack of my life chapters are now most audible and poignant.

The ghost of the past is sitting dark and solemn on the seat opposite me. It is waiting for my confession; I know this, feel it. Just a few miles away resides Murphy. He stares from a bay window of his beautiful home at a train passing. I pass; we are both conscious of our historic back drop. He stands proud and successful; at ease with himself, a stranger.

I surmise that my existence at the back of the minds of James and Murphy is of a child who never really grew up. I will always remain the guy who tried too hard, the person who liked blues and beer, sex and food, swimming and reading; always swimming against the tide, constantly trying to understand literature that was far to intellectual for a secondary school kid.

But, because I was cognisant during my late teens and early adulthood of my naivety and intellectual shortcomings, I continued in solitude to study; too late in the day, I found that I could hold a conversation across a wide variety of subjects with the most self-opinionated raconteur. I have come to the conclusion that *memory* is vital to obtaining academic skills. I have a poor memory. Creativity however is not necessarily memory dependant. I always did well when my exams were based upon course work, poor results reflected my weakness of memory, formula, historic dates, quotations etc.

The fact that I write this short confession/ autobiography should reassure me that at 64.5 years old I have not given up, never ceased from questioning and stretching my mind so as to eliminate the risk of further humiliation in company.

The drink is getting darker. Outside of this shed window is a whole grey world. The whole grey world is lost. It drifts with billions of self-aware folk who believe in various gods and political systems. These humans are mostly made up of mutineers and dreamers. No matter what poets and philosophers scribe, the planet, as far as mankind is concerned, is dying of cancer.

My wife of 39 years is working. I am dreaming and typing, imagining and typing, typing and drinking, drinking and typing, that's all, biding time, waiting for curtains to breeze across a stage, the stage waits for another naive soul to tread timber and express themselves in the limelight of Johns powerful Apocalypse.

I have prepared supper. My wife, my rock of reality suffers the strangeness. Our children long since flown the strangeness settle far away in their nests of fortune. And my arms are not long enough to embrace. I miss their wriggles. Miss the detritus of their existence. Miss the time disciplines of schooling and of setting an example.

There is, just outside the shed a solitary daffodil, its external leaves are brown, and its head is bowed down. It will never see summer.

The shed has no door.

There once was a group. Their collective name is Espers, mostly acoustic soul searching stuff, terrific female vocals. I was led to these guys by a track from Marianne Faithful's album "Easy Come Easy Go" track name "Children of Stone" I love the way strong messages span the years, Faithfull does justice to this most poetic lament…all that blossoms, all that blooms lies fallow in the night"

I don't know if I shall return to write more. But of this I am sure. The blues for me, those minor chords and string bending screams have helped me exhale all my innermost pent up emotions for many years. They have helped as a pressure release valve does on a pressure cooker…..helped me survive the heat of inter human competitiveness that desensitises those who possess sensitivity.

Long Live naivety, long live ignorance!

Without these two voids, creativity would suffocate.

But now, there is some dark treacle...

And like a short sweaty dream a month has passed by. I am drawn back to this keyboard by sun, alcohol, sheer bloody mindedness and drink. I have come across a young lady guitarist (wishful thinking), her initials E Z. She is page three, blonde, hour glass figure…oh! And her playing is out of this world; there being no music of hers on Amazon I am playing her youtube postings to death. I am either envious of her youth, good looks, and musical acumen or it's something deeper.

She will be playing on a stage long after I have left mine. I love being in the kitchen in this party of life, it is so damn hard to open the door into the darkness. Resting, steaming in his cd case is another new find, Doyle Bramhill 11. His playing is powerful, how did I find him? Roger Waters' album "In the Flesh" has a DVD, the track "Comfortably Numb" shows this young guy playing like a genius, I look at the credits, oh damn he is so young and good looking, the Earth is now so old and has ugly masses. There are angels that tingle flesh at the edge of feedback.

My circle of friends has diminished substantially. For a bloke with many ailments and wrinkles, I drink and try to prove to myself that I can still handle it….big mistake. I am bricking myself into this shed. Every time I visit it another brick another plank is secured. I am constantly running downstream to prove that *I* can step into the same river twice.

It is hard to leave a person you love, heart-breaking to leave a place one loves. Outside the shed I sit at an old circular pub table waiting…waiting for my wife to return from work. I sit a watch dancing midges. I can smell the fecundity of this virgin summer, I can hear the chorus of agitated birds and the plop of basking canal fish, I can taste my liquid apples, touch the coarse dry leaves of sage…its fucking good…too fucking good.

Images of long lost friends flash through my mind. Briefly passes an old buddy who came on board my life many years ago whilst I was flying a radio controlled plane. I was not long at work and full of sexual thoughts. My plane (I had finished it in black solarfilm) had wings adorned with large letters giving the model a name "Sex Machine!" The title was also a best-selling and much played track by James Brown in our local disco-The Elms Hotel in Aldridge. We danced "The Bump" to this classic. A young chap came over to me and asked if I would take his model up for a spin and trim out as he had never flown radio before.

I obliged and took Peter's plane up into the air, put it through a few manoeuvres, landed it safely and congratulated him on the quality of his first build. Over the following weeks and months he quickly picked up the skill of model flying. We often went for a few beers, we seemed to have a lot in common, and it turned out that this was not the case at all. I liked the guy a lot. There was however a strong reticence in his attitude regarding friendship. It was obvious that as long as I was of some use to him he was around. Peter played his cards so close to his chest that he could never see them himself. He catches friends and pins them like unfeeling taxi rides from life node to life node. He returns now in my mind because he recently touched my robe when he was floundering and has since recovered his balance and gone. I can get very passionate when it comes to friendship. I hate with a vehement fire folk who use others as stepping stones without a backward glance. I hunger for retribution when friends and family fail to reciprocate integrity of character. My Father and Peter are such animals. They spark to life the Black Dog that resides in me. I don't want anyone to dry my feet. I long for a calmer and more sedate life of late. I am tired of second guessing others hidden agendas and schemes.

***

From the Shed window I see a garden then a vision of my Aunt. In the mid to late sixties pocket money was rare. I was 14, needed street cred Wrangler Jeans and Cheese cloth shirts. My aunt was a beautiful slim film star of a woman. She, my mother's sister, was vibrant and sassy. She drove a door to door bakers van. She gave me pocket money for helping her run up and down driveways and flat stairs (I was on large quantities of steroids then) delivering loaves and cakes to a good cross section of homes.

She seemed to be on my side back then, all for the hippy genre and I used to confide stuff. My naivety was at a high in those days. Sometimes she would leave me in a café with beans and toast, put four records on the juke box, Beatles, Kinks, whatever. She told me on lots of occasions during our tear about Walsall…

"I have to drive to meet up with Bob on another round…you'd like bob Steve…we are short on tarts and bloomers, he always has spare stuff!"

Eventually I met Bob…he was older than my Aunt, a sort of aged Spaniard type. He smoked heavily… and he seemed better company than my Uncle who hardly, then, acknowledged my existence - treated me as if I was invisible. He made my Aunt laugh and she would place her hands in prayer style between her hippy thighs as she was seated in the café and roared with laughter at his jokes until she joked exclaiming “stop it I will wet myself!” .

One wet and hot dogging day…she was taking a long time returning to pick me up from the café. I was skint, no more songs playing from the juke box all at once the cafe became a wall paper peeling waiting room. I was looking forward to my ten bob note (50p). I decided to walk outside and take a look up and down the street for her bakers van. I didn’t have far to walk.

It was parked just around the corner close to the curb. Its windows steamed up with rain. By the look on her blushed face, she had been crying.

I wanted my Aunt to find happiness. I never found out why she didn’t have children. I surmised that maybe her generosity toward me was a substitute that she hungered for a child. I couldn’t help this.

It has only been recently, the last couple of years-8 in all that I have come to grow cold when thinking about my beautiful Aunt. My father and I it seemed; were unpopular for putting my mother (the eldest of the family) into a dementia home. The Aunt gave me a hard time, constantly slamming the phone down mid-sentence until I could not tolerate the stuff further. So ended a chapter in my young life story; trying for years to come to terms with my mother’s demise and my father’s frailty, I never had the chance to make amends or explain decisions that had apparently so upset her.

And the garden returns to my vision, as if I was on a death bed and flashes of life sketches plumage in my mind. The shed is now playing a track called “Blame” by Doyle Bramhall 11.

I am suddenly overcome with anxiety. I stand, I sit, I am confused and I fear for my sanity, I am alone. My being consists of ethereal music waves which are drifting in and out of ivy wrapped rafters. I hang on to my workbench but I am a fly in a match box, yes a fly in a matchbox being rattled about, before me the shed window, this is my vision to the outside world. Behind me the shed wall hangs with posters of past blues stars. To my right is the door through which I was born and to the left a solid un-negotiable gable end of death. I look down at the computer. The word count is never enough to satiate my absolute wish for creativity. I have fucking run out of time. My life dough will never rise, never.

I realise that there is a *clear and present danger* of ruining the supper. I cannot move, I see the kitchen window - steamed up. There are hands between thighs, and sins in tins, secrets in supressed passion. I cannot move; I want to draw attention to my plight. I am lost. Nobody knows I am here, and I have no means to transmit my co-ordinates.

This madness isn't funny anymore. The CD is repeating itself, time is standing still, a sparrow waves its wings to awaken me but I am lost, sinking fast, I am drowning in chords, the sharps the majors and minors…a living death.

Ah! The Blues, when it strikes, the possibilities of pulling the trigger are acute.

***

My wife is an enigma. She was half my weight when we met. Her dresses and skirts freely danced around her petite body. Her breasts- for the first 38 years of marriage are the only things I would, in confidence, be able to identify her by. She has been, since our inception my guardian angel. She gave me a most precious gift, a gift so rare that it is priceless.

"FREEDOM".

I have never heard her whinge and moan…

I have never had a complaint or been scolded.

She has put up with years of me dominating the car and house audio equipment.

She can be caught laughing *like some sublime message* behind her hand at my vision; a mature man playing an air guitar, wriggling my torso like Hendrix. I know she does this...and it's a good grounder.

She gave birth to four wonderful children. I was the first. In my letter to her in response to the lonely hearts advert, I said a few things about my temperament which would have put off most enquirers. From the seven replies I received, I chose hers. I chose Elaine's letter and chose Elaine for the journey. Her letter was written in a most dainty unpretentious non bull shitting style that I felt I knew her already. I saw it in her eyes. "Give him enough rope………

Throughout our marriage I have hung myself many times. She has religiously stood by me, removed pegs from my ears, and placed me on a windowsill to dry in *her* sun. When one is possessed with an over active creativity gland, selfishness runs from the eyes. It blinds one from seeing anxiety in the faces of those we love.

Our table tennis humour goes along these lines…

<u>Steve</u>

Don't you think you have enough bags, including the ones under your eyes!

<u>Elaine</u>

At least I'm not a late developer!

We are a team; a team which is now exhausted with the journey. Each day we make allowances for each other. The dust on our wings has been brushed off by the ripples of duty and compassion. With each disappointment of expectation we adjust our guide ropes. Things become taught. We become harder and less tolerant. Appointments are kept rigidly. Friends peel away, snubbed at our refusals and excuses for not coming out to play. We grow weary of work. Weary of the same old drudge; tired of worrying about our children and our impotence when it comes to caring for aged parents. We are husks of our former selves. We have nothing left to offer. I lie. We have a couple of attributes that may be of value-an example of staying power and roots. This is the only credit we have to offer at the feet of older and younger family members.

My last stage of love of the Blues has been reached. We recently attended an evening of live blues at our local venue, Robin 2 at Bilston. There was a young man and his Band, Grant Pritchard. He saved his best guitar solo until the last -they were supporting Chantel McGregor. Pritchard gave a fine performance of Voodoo Chile (Hendrix). We waited until 9.30 for Chantel McGregor and her band came onto stage. Wifey and I had both been working and were wilting at this point. Mc Gregor began with a few acoustic songs, snatched up her electric guitar and proceeded to excel any feedback performance ever achieved (in my opinion) by Hendrix and Trower. I hate to admit this but she totally blew away the old and welcomed in the new. No matter what art you may be gifted with, yes it's unique, however its genre will be stretched.

I listened to this very young Guitarist as she ripped open the hearts of many a twilight guy stage pressed and camera poised. There is life after Hendrix, and on stage-living proof. Aged folk of both sexes played air guitar and long to death their wishes to live life again and follow like rats to the sound of a Fender being played by a girl. A track and I may be wrong called Inconsolable (unlisted on her repertoire) was strangled from her sound system until the most stoical of music philosophers gasped with orgasmic passion when she ceased and smiled. There was a lot to come, but for me and the sight of my wife's tired eyes, it was the time to go. We rolled away from Chantel an hour early and enjoyed a smoking bag of chips and early to bed. We left the blues girl to convince others, we were already sold.

So energy drains away with old age. The passion still resides in the heart. With every negative humanitarian report on the media the blues kicks in. From downright ignorance shown by politicians in respect to the needs of a common man, to the murderous thoughts of terrorists and revolutionaries, the blues acts as a pressure valve, anger somewhat placated by the sacrifices and lyrics of wailing souls. Hendrix culminated this wrath with his track Machine Gun. Back then in the seventies the birth of modern technology; I swapped my wind up watch for a digital, my log book and slide rule for a calculator. We were then fed up of the IRA bombs, pissed off with the Middle East and we younger folk began to question what we were being asked to believe. This has now come to a head with the democratic vote to leave the comfort of the European Union and re-establish interest in self-belief. Ok a forty year gap…never argue with someone who has absolutely nothing to lose.

***

PART 2

I chuckle to myself. The shed is hot; the reason for the chuckle? I have invented a method of pulling teeth without anaesthetic. Could save NHS millions, and make private practitioners millionaires.

Transindental Medication.

A balmy night approaches. Just a few miles away in separate dwellings…one costing £1k per week, the other costing the price of a scrooges ransom, loneliness, lie my Mother and father and this situation is in its 8th year and I am 100 years old tonight because I've had enough of the whole caring shit...which is just an unloving chore. The chore manifests itself in a sense of military duty, a sense of not letting the system down, being the only child, doing stuff like walking in water drenched clay, or trying to placate a spoilt child without striking out.

Outside, the dusk of a terrorism flavoured world closes in. The shed door rattles and scrapes for attention at rusty hinges. Colder fronts thermalize the sultry air as she blows kisses to me to waken my senses.

I am almost sick at the sudden manifestation of a ghostly vision. From the shed window, I behold a vision of a human dressed in black. Its face looks at me from under a pagan hood. The face is half woman half man, and even so it is a beautiful vision a true delight to the eye. I wave in acknowledgement at the advancing figure. I stand and push past the oscillating shed door to greet the stranger, this manifestation… S-me-M-Manifestation.

S Hi, do I know you?, how the fuck you get in here?

M Steve, don't be alarmed. Go…go back into your cocoon and sit down, it's time we had a chat.

S Oh shit, is this it, death?

M you died years ago, you know that, don't come the innocent ignoramus…

S I don't get it,

M We are "you" Steve - a culmination of all your aspirations.

S Ok…and?

M Its time to remodel, now sit at your computer you won't remember, we have started this for you…

S You want me to take notes? record this…I'm pissed, you are.

M Pissed….lets laugh…

S I only hear the masculine…..

M Exactly….you are catching on…we use the vernacular…the best you have…

S I want to hear her, the other side of you…

M And that's where the problem lies.

S Point of view?

M No, dominance, you're male biased.

S I am a male, what the fuck are you doing here? Why isn't *she* talking?

M We are the culmination of all your aspirations…

S Slow learner…

M Indeed

S I can't write about what I cannot feel.

M Bollocks! You drink heavily, you have blotted out half of your potential; a nature given gift was bestowed upon you…and since you watched a James Cagney film, you have worn waistcoats, toted plastic machine guns and rescued the blonde!

S I always wished for a Bonnie and Clyde existence…so sexy.

M Sexy if both sexes are represented equally.

S Will she talk to me…the gorgeous side of your face?

M When you acknowledge *her* aspirations, you're almost there. She is just one sentence away from talking to you. Please write it and read it out loud, scream it out. She is waiting.

I see a tear in the corner of her eye she makes no move to capture its diamond. I look into her eye, and realise what I have done.

It is dark now, the darkness has swallowed them up, devoured their robes like black leaf cutter bees scissoring the petals of roses.

Bugger, I shall not be satisfied until I have found the sentence that will undo all the injustices woven into my 100 years of treachery.

I have limited time to make amends. The culmination of aspiration spirit has made a death bed appeal, it is lodged now in my heart and I accept the quest.

I accept the quest.

Spirit of the Blues and of Nature I hope you will guide me to the sentence.

There is Something in the Air (Thunderclap Newman).

***

I think. I think too much and wish I didn't lead this life of characters. Analogy; I purchased a Tibetan singing bowl. It took my eye in a pagan shop. It is solid brass and is beautifully perfect, very expensive. So I picked it up and pushed past a myriad of dimly lit cobwebs and screaming silent artefacts…

"hi, I will take this!" I demanded of the Welsh Druidess

"Don't you want to hear it?" she said to the half pagan in the half light.

I felt such a fraud. All the reading I had done Plato, Pirsig Hulme, Spinoza,…"Shit" I have fell for the aesthetic trap…forgot the soul, the sound…and now I am repeating my ignorance, writing in the male tongue…a quest to write with feeling a sentence that will pay tribute to my Goddess.

I tapped the edge of the singing bowl with the wooden pestle. The bowl sounded dull.

"Sir!" hold it like this!" said the druid balancing the brass bowl on a tripod of her fingers.

She tapped the bowl with the tree splinter and the thing hummed so sweetly and with such deep meaning I was transfixed.

The bowl was handed back to me. I hit her with the timber and she sang and the vibrations soothed my ignorance because it was a sound of light and enlightenment.

Tibetan singing bowl has gathered dust in our lounge for 29 years now.

And now it all makes perfect sense. Somehow during my transformation from young to old adulthood I had become pre-occupied with survival. Missing the trick, not understanding the joke, ignoring the good things around me, letting them gather dust, seeing things at face value-ignoring the fucking gift.

I stop here. I stop writing…I am urgently skipping and gambolling from the shed to the Tibetan. I am going to beat and silk slide a whole angelic *come* outa the fucking thing…fuck what the neighbours think, I will use my wooden finger to circle the rim slowly and bring her dusty presence back to life again with a body blow orgasm.

Then my mind returns from the spectre of imagination.

I sit in the shed on a pile of my own embers of thoughts, my passion spent.

I look around the shed for something new and my eye catches something old. Kant. Silly old Kant; the book I tug is slim and is a summary of Kant and his work by Paul Strathern. I tug again and a whole pile of thoughts tumble in a damp and dusty mess across the floor. The cover and pages are dull, heavily laden with hay fever and allergy powder. Around the book edges hang grandmother's hair cobwebs and carapace carcases, the remains of some horror movie 8 legged redips lunch. The texture of the book leaves me somewhat reluctant to open it, fearing what's inside.

Opened; the book has obviously gone through some serious criticism by me. Heavily underlined, frisked and asterisked.

Here are some examples:-

Kant's inability (or unwillingness) to form close relationships was indicative of a profound unhappiness.

Friendship is a restriction of favourable sentiments to a single subject and is very pleasant to whomsoever they are directed, but also proof that generality and goodwill are lacking.

A priori, don't know? Look up, knowledge gained from reasoning and theoretical deduction rather than from human observation.

We should act in accordance with our duty and not our feelings.

Never tell a lie regardless of consequences…… BOLLOCKS!
Describing something as beautiful is demanding other people see the same………Crap!...personal observation...

20 years ago I ploughed through the writings of philosophers to get the damn stuff out of my system. I have been dabbling in it since I was a teenager. I regret that I never attended formal teaching on the subject. The desire to master a subject has haunted me until it is too late. I play guitar but have no confidence to learn music. I can pick up discarded or resting axes in pubs and entertain folk for a few moments. I have many hundreds of albums and can pick a track at the drop of a mood; raising or diminishing the spirit. I contemplated being a disc jockey… local station another pipemare.

The search for the lost chord is exhausting. Back in the sixties I was all fire and water - looking for some rich bastard's nymphomaniac daughter. She could pour single malt onto my flames.

I set my sights too high which resulted in depression and my recognising the same.

My father objected to me going to art school. He wanted me to start work in a foundry; a dirty hole where he worked including my Grandfather before him.

It was confirmed that I was tone deaf.

I would have done better to start with shooting myself in the foot.

The Vine, my local pub where everyone knows who to blame was today teaming with bar mechanics.

A barmaid nicknamed Sweep, has complete control. She is young tattooed and slim, a twiglet.

I asked if she would like to have children.

"What? Who wants to push a fucking pineapple through a polo mint?"

I started off drinking in the sixties in such pubs. I am hanging on to the few that are left. Pubs like this are falling like dominoes. They are living jigsaws of life that have no pieces missing. There's always someone who is better at telling jokes, has had sex with more partners than anyone else, the whole rough pub atmosphere is built like some layer cake. Unorthodox strangers are lab samples for the sly lonely; the beer dwelling property provides a family home for misfits.

My taste in music is mellowing. I remain a fan of the golden voiced poet Leonard Cohen. His philosophical lyrics and slow deliberating delivery is so comforting. His masterpiece Live in London recorded at the O2 Arena in July 2008 is a recent purchase. It is now 2016. Eight years ago I was struggling with parental problems, kept putting off the buying of this album. Whether or not listening to him eight years ago would have made any difference in my mental state-nursing the hatred of seeing my parents and myself in aging decline, is superfluous. I hear the aged singer now. It is final curtain stuff. The time has come and I realise I have given life my best shot. It is time to stand back and look at the portrait. I know that if I hate what I see, it will not be because of the lack of art school training, or my tone deafness; but a failure to realise that I had indeed stumbled upon an amazon. If I hate my self-portrait it will be because it has been painted by a naïve beer swilling hedonistic dreamer who traipsed through music shops like a bull in a china shop. If however I can reason my way out of the enigmatic vision, there will be, in a corner of the picture an Angel. The androgynous spectre that visited me needs a big thank you, the words are:-

Wifey I Love You.

Epilogue

Following a lot of reading and writing 2003-2009, I obtained a BA degree. The struggle in a competitive world, with limited amount of money and intelligence was worth the sacrifice. I felt extremely anxious and guilty at taking money from our family income to pursue this goal. Having achieved recognition in education at the age of 57 although it hasn't been a financial benefit in any way, I can stand next to my educated and hardworking friends without too much humility. My advice is to chisel away at insecurities and listen to intuition. Never turn a stranger from your door. Don't burn bridges. I have loved you all.

The End

www.ingramcontent.com/pod-product-compliance
Ingram Content Group UK Ltd.
Pitfield, Milton Keynes, MK11 3LW, UK
UKHW042001190726
13854UKWH00005B/2110

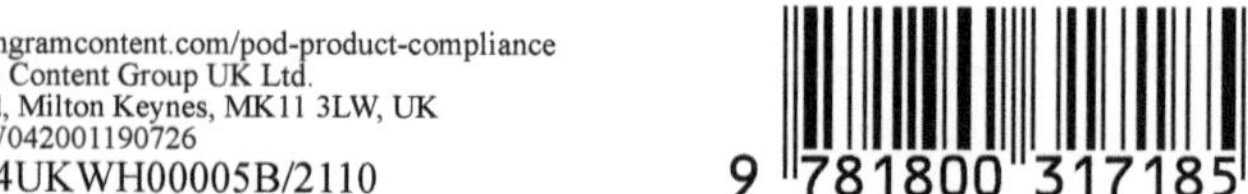

9 781800 317185